EARLY HOURS, ENDLESS POWER:
OWNING YOUR MORNING, TRANSFORMING YOUR LIFE.

CYNTHIA A. EDWARDS.

TABLE OF CONTENT.

INTRODUCTION.

THE MORNING REVOLUTION.

Some time ago, in a little, honest town, there carried on with a young fellow named Alex.

He was a conventional person with a remarkable dream — to have an effect on the planet. Yet, in the same way as other of us, Alex frequently ended up trapped in the constant tornado of life, as though he were being cleared along by a wild current.

One night, as he sat alone in his faintly lit loft, contemplating the great vision he had for his life, a disclosure struck him like a bat out of hell. It wasn't the terrific motions or the inestimable fortuitous events that planned to lead him to his predetermination; it was the basic, regular demonstration of getting up right on time.

Alex chose to leave on an excursion of self-disclosure, an excursion that would before long lead him to a significant acknowledgment — an acknowledgment that would change his life until the end of time.

He named this excursion "The Morning Unrest."

As the main beams of daylight kissed the skyline the following morning, Alex rose from his bed, sooner than he ever had previously. With a feeling of assurance that had been stirred inside him, he found that these early hours held the way to opening his actual potential. They were the point at which the world was still, and interruptions were at least, leaving space for profound reflection and centered activity.

"The Morning Insurgency," he thought, "isn't just about getting up right on time; it's tied in with releasing the full degree of our true capacity during those valuable hours when the world rests."

As he dove further into this freshly discovered venture, Alex figured out how to make a morning schedule that invigorated his body and brain, supported his efficiency, sustained his spirit, and, in particular, supported the change. He started to observe a significant change in his life. The straightforward demonstration of dominating his initial hours had touched off a progression of striking changes.

CHAPTER 1.

RISE AND SPARKLE.

The Significance of Morning dominance.

The morning hours are not only a period to sluggishly awaken, race through your daily practice, and go to work or school. They are a unimaginable chance to establish the vibe until the end of your day and, thus, your life. We should investigate the meaning of morning predominance.

- Figuring out the force of your Morning Schedule.

Envision a normal morning:

You shock alert, frightened by your booming morning timer. You nap it a couple of times until you hesitantly drag yourself up, racing to get dressed and plan for the day ahead. Sound natural? This is a routine a large number of us are excessively acquainted with, yet it's nowhere near powerful. The most important move towards morning predominance is understanding the power of your morning plan.

1. The Force of Expectation: Mornings can be tumultuous, yet they can likewise be snapshots of calm and expectation. By

assuming command over your morning plan, you can lay out an underpinning of direction for the day ahead. Rather than racing through your morning, envision making a quiet standard that makes way for a useful day.

- Work out: Attempt this activity. Envision a morning where you awaken very much refreshed, do a touch of extending, contemplate or peruse, and partake in a sustaining breakfast prior to beginning your work. Presently envision a morning where you hit the nap button on various occasions, race to prepare, skip breakfast, and rush out the entryway. Which morning could you like?

2. A Diagram for Progress: Your morning resembles the plan for an effective day. A very much organized morning schedule can guarantee you start the day feeling good, engaged, and spurred.

- Reflection: Pause for a minute to ponder your ongoing morning schedule. What does it resemble? Is it viable in setting you up for the day ahead? What components might you at any point improve or acquaint with make it more deliberate?

3. Extraordinary Potential: Mornings hold extraordinary potential. They give an open door to self-awareness, taking care of oneself, and purposeful objective setting. By assuming responsibility for your mornings, you can saddle this potential and set up for a life changing change.

- Objective Setting: Think about defining a particular objective for your mornings. It very well may be essentially as straightforward as getting up 30 minutes sooner, or as aggressive as integrating reflection, work out, and a nutritious breakfast into your everyday practice. The key is to begin with attainable advances.

4. Uncover Your Enthusiasm: Mornings can be an opportunity to reconnect with your interests and interests. With more command over your timetable, you can apportion time to seek after exercises that give you pleasure and satisfaction.

- Activity Steps: Contemplate an action you're enthusiastic about however frequently lack the capacity to deal with because of your hurried mornings. Whether it's perusing, painting, playing an instrument, or just partaking in a comfortable mug of espresso, recognize how you can integrate it into your morning schedule.

- Making Way for Change

Now that we've investigated the power of your morning plan, the following stage is to clear a path for change. Changing your mornings and, thusly, your life requires a readiness to embrace change and new propensities.

1. Embracing Change: Change can be both energizing and overwhelming. Moving toward change with a receptive outlook and an uplifting perspective is significant. Consider your morning schedule a material for change.

- Mentality Shift: Think about your ongoing mentality towards mornings. Do you fear them, or do you anticipate the conceivable outcomes they bring? Changing your mentality towards mornings can be the most vital phase in making enduring enhancements.

2. Little Advances, Huge Effect: Change doesn't need to be extraordinary. It's generally expected more powerful when it's continuous, truth be told. Little, reliable advances can prompt huge changes after some time.

- Activity Plan: Make an activity plan for change. Begin with a basic change, like getting up 15 minutes sooner, and continuously work from that point. The key is to roll out the improvement supportable.

3. Responsibility and Backing: Change is simpler when you have backing and responsibility. Consider including a companion or relative in your morning schedule to help each other keep focused.

- Responsibility Accomplice: Find somebody who shares your objectives and will consider you responsible. You can check in with one another everyday or week after week to keep tabs on your development and give inspiration.

4. Perception and Attestations: Picture the change you need to find in your mornings and your life. Make positive insistences that mirror your ideal morning schedule and rehash them everyday.

- Representation Exercise: Shut your eyes and envision your optimal morning schedule. What does it resemble? How would you feel during this everyday practice? Representation can be an incredible asset for showing change.

By understanding the power of your morning timetable and accounting for change, you can leave on an excursion towards morning predominance, where your mornings become the springboard for a more intentional and satisfying life.

The Study of Early Rising

Now that we've investigated the meaning of morning predominance, we should plunge into the science behind early ascending in "The Investigation of Early Rising." This part gives the information and understanding important to arrive at informed conclusions about your morning schedule.

- Circadian Rhythms and Rest Examples

1. ** The Body's Inside Clock:** The human body works on a characteristic circadian cadence, which is basically a 24-hour organic clock. This clock impacts different physiological cycles, including rest and wake designs. Circadian rhythms are controlled by outer signs like light and temperature,

however they additionally differ from one individual to another.

- Grasping Your Cadence: Begin by focusing on your normal rest designs. Is it true or not that you are normally an early riser or an evening person? Understanding your remarkable circadian musicality can assist you with fitting your morning schedule to your body's inclinations.

2. The Rest Wake Cycle: Our circadian rhythms impact the rest wake cycle. At the point when your body's inner clock lines up with your day to day daily practice, you experience better rest quality and more energy during waking hours.

- Trial and error: Explore different avenues regarding adjusting your rest wake cycle with your optimal morning schedule. Steadily change your sleep time and wake-up opportunity to perceive what it means for your energy and efficiency.

3. The Job of Melatonin: Melatonin is a chemical delivered by the pineal organ in light of haziness. It assumes a urgent part in managing the rest wake cycle. Understanding melatonin can assist you with upgrading your rest.

- Light Openness: Be aware of your openness to counterfeit light, particularly at night. An excessive amount of counterfeit light can stifle melatonin creation and impede your rest cycle. Consider darkening lights at night and keeping away from screens before sleep time.

● Delivering Your Normal Energy.
Morning Cortisol: Cortisol, frequently alluded to as the "stress chemical," assumes a

huge part in our mornings. It normally increments in the first part of the day to help us awaken and perk up.

Solid Pressure Management: While cortisol has a terrible standing, it's fundamental for awakening and getting rolling.

CHAPTER 2.

BUILDING YOUR MORNING SCHEDULE.

Your morning plan is the outline for your day. It establishes the vibe for your efficiency, energy, and in general prosperity. In this part, we'll investigate how to make a morning schedule that enables you to handle your day head-on.

Mind Over Nap Button: Beating Morning Hindrances.

Picture this situation:

Your alert goes off in the first part of the day, and everything you believe should do is raised a ruckus around town button. You're in good company. Large numbers of us face these morning obstacles. Be that as it may, in this part, we'll examine how to vanquish them and take full advantage of your mornings.

- Overcoming the Enticement of Rest

- Perceiving the Enticement: It's critical to recognize the charm of remaining in bed somewhat longer, particularly when you're comfortable and warm. The rest button appears as though an alarm's call. However, recollect, it's generally expected a transitory joy that can prompt more tiredness and surged mornings.

- Reflection: Pause for a minute to contemplate the times you've yielded to the enticement of napping. What did it cost you regarding investment? How is it that that could time have been exceptional spent?

- Setting Different Cautions: On the off chance that you're a chronic snoozer, take a stab at setting cautions at various spots in your room, compelling you to get up to switch them off. This actual activity can assist with getting out from under the propensity.

- Deliberate Arousing: Rethink your outlook around awakening. Rather than considering it a commitment, consider it to be an open door. This psychological shift can be a strong inspiration.

- Getting through Mental Obstructions.

- Morning Uneasiness: Many individuals experience morning nervousness, which can make it trying to get up. Understanding the wellspring of this uneasiness and carrying out methodologies to ease it can have a major effect.

- Care Practices: Integrating care strategies into your morning schedule can assist with mitigating morning nervousness. Basic breathing activities or a short contemplation can make a quiet and focused mentality.

- Preparing: In some cases, the nervousness is connected to ineptness for the afternoon. Making a plan for the day or setting out what you want for the morning can diminish this psychological barrier.

- Reward Framework: Execute a little prize framework for yourself toward the beginning of the day. It very well may be pretty much as straightforward as partaking in some your #1 tea or espresso after you complete your morning schedule. This can give inspiration to defeat mental checks.

Designing your optimal Morning schedule.

Now that we've talked about beating morning preventions, now is the right time to plan your ideal morning plan. A very much organized morning schedule is your clear-cut advantage for a useful day.

- Creating Your Own Morning Outline.

- Self-Reflection: Begin by thinking about your own inclinations and what exercises cause you to feel your best in the first part of the day. Everybody's ideal morning will appear to be unique.

- Action Appraisal: List the exercises that empower and persuade you toward the beginning of the day. It very well may be perusing, working out, journaling, or essentially partaking in a comfortable breakfast.

- Redoing Your Everyday practice: With your rundown of favored exercises close by, begin fabricating your morning schedule. Consider how long you really want for each and what request seems OK for you.

- Fitting your daily schedules to your objectives.

- Arrangement with Objectives: Your morning schedule ought to line up with your day to day targets and long haul objectives. If you have any desire to work on your wellness, for instance, integrate practice into your morning plan.

- Objective Setting: Pause for a minute to lay out clear objectives for your morning schedule. Whether it's rising efficiency, decreasing pressure, or supporting your imagination, your routine ought to be custom-made to accomplish these objectives.

- Using time effectively: Take advantage of your time by grasping your pinnacle long stretches of efficiency. Assuming you're most ready toward the beginning of the day, focus on your most significant assignments during this time.

Nutrition and hydration: Power for your morning.

Legitimate sustenance and hydration are fundamental for a fruitful morning schedule. They give the fuel your body needs to launch the day.

- The Morning meal of Champions

- Significance of Breakfast: Breakfast is many times promoted as the main dinner of the day, and justifiably. It refuels your body and cerebrum following a night's rest.

- Adjusted Nourishment: Guarantee your morning meal incorporates an equilibrium of protein, complex starches, and sound fats. This blend gives supported energy and keeps you feeling full longer.

- Feast Planning: Think about setting up some morning meal parts the prior night to save time. Short-term oats, smoothie packs, or pre-cut natural product can smooth out your morning schedule.

- Staying Hydrated for Ideal Execution.

- Lack of hydration Effect: Lack of hydration can prompt weariness and diminished mental capability. Beginning your day with a glass of water can help launch your digestion and give a psychological and actual lift.

- Hydration Update: Put a glass of water on your end table before bed to remind you to hydrate when you awaken. You can likewise set hourly updates on your telephone to guarantee you're drinking sufficient water over the course of the day.

- Hydration Tips: Try different things with adding new lemon or cucumber cuts to your water for a reviving turn. Home grown teas and mixed water are additionally superb decisions for hydration.

- Careful Eating: Practice careful having during breakfast. Enjoy each nibble, and be available at the time. This can establish an inspirational vibe until the end of your day.

By tending to morning obstructions, planning a customized morning schedule, and understanding the meaning of sustenance and hydration, you're well headed to building a strong morning plan that can change your day to day existence.

CHAPTER 3.

CHANGING YOUR LIFE.

Leaving on an excursion of change requires a complex methodology. In this segment, we will dive into the psychological, physical, and reasonable parts of completely changing yourself to accomplish your ideal objectives.

Mindset Makeover: Developing Energy and Efficiency.

Your outlook is a useful asset that can either frustrate or work with individual change. We should investigate the parts of a mentality makeover.

- The Force of Positive Reasoning.

1. Figuring out the Force of Positive Reasoning.

- The Psyche Body Association: Positive reasoning isn't just about pie in the sky considerations; it substantially affects your body and prosperity. At the point when you think decidedly, your body discharges endorphins, the "vibe great" chemicals that can help your temperament and energy levels.

- Viable Activity: Attempt this down to earth work out. Begin your day by posting three things you're appreciative for. Consider how this exercise causes you to feel. The force of appreciation can establish an inspirational vibe for your morning.

- Objective Setting and perception.

    - Lucidity of Goals: Defining clear objectives is fundamental for change. At the point when you understand what you need to accomplish, it becomes simpler to structure your activities and roll out the important improvements.

    - Shrewd Objectives: Utilize the Shrewd models for objective setting: Explicit, Quantifiable, Attainable, Important, and Time-bound. For instance, rather than an unclear objective like "I need to get better," you could lay out a Brilliant objective like "I will practice for 30 minutes each day to further develop my wellness level in three months or less."

- Representation: Envisioning your objectives can assist with making them a reality. Put shortly every early daytime imagining yourself prevailing in your goals. This training can upgrade inspiration and assurance.

Exercise and development: Invigorating Your Morning.

Actual work is an intense device for improving your morning and, thus, your life. We should investigate how exercise can fortify your morning schedule.

- Integrating Active work

- Move to Invigorate: Taking part in some type of active work toward the beginning of the day can give a quick jolt of energy. It very well may be a lively walk, yoga, extending, or a full exercise. The key is to get your blood streaming and increment oxygen supply to your mind.

- Activity Step: Cause a rundown of proactive tasks you to appreciate or might want to attempt in the first part of the day. It very well may be basically as straightforward as a 10-minute extending normal or a 30-minute exercise. Try different things with various exercises to see what invigorates you the most.

- The advantages of Morning exercises.

- Begin the Day Solid: Morning exercise upgrades your actual wellbeing as well as your psychological and close to home prosperity. It establishes an uplifting vibe for the afternoon, increments readiness, and lessens pressure.

- Consistency: By practicing in the first part of the day, you lay out a steady normal that is less inclined to be disturbed by startling occasions later in the day.

- Digestion Lift: Morning activity can fire up your digestion, assisting you with consuming more calories over the course of the day. It's an extraordinary approach to launch your day, both with regards to energy and actual wellness.

- Profound Flexibility: Morning exercise has been displayed to deliver endorphins, which are normal temperament lifters. This can assist you with confronting difficulties with a more certain outlook.

- Further developed Rest: Shockingly, morning activity can add to all the more likely rest quality. It directs your circadian cadence, prompting more peaceful evenings.

- Activity Plan: Focus on adding activity to your morning schedule. Begin with a sensible span and continuously increment it. Whether it's a home exercise, a run, or yoga, pick an action that impacts you.

Productivity hacks for Morning People.

Efficiency is the way to accomplishing your objectives and changing your life. How about we investigate a few down to earth procedures to support your morning productivity.

- Time Usage Techniques.

1. Early daytime Arranging

- Prioritization: Before your day starts, require a couple of moments to focus on your undertakings. Recognize the most significant and dire ones, and plan your morning schedule appropriately.

- Time Impeding: Time obstructing includes planning explicit blocks of time for various assignments. Apportion centered time for fundamental exercises, like profound work, exercise, and breakfast.

2. Limit Interruptions.

- Advanced Detox: Limit your openness to computerized interruptions in the first part of the day. Try not to browse messages or web-based entertainment until you've finished your most significant responsibilities.

- Make an Interruption Free Space: Assign a particular region for work or study where you can concentrate without interferences.

- Quietness or Music: Explore different avenues regarding foundation commotion. Certain individuals work better peacefully, while others find delicate instrumental music or repetitive sound for fixation.

- Activity Step: Attempt time obstructing for your morning schedule. Dispense explicit time allotments for various exercises, and adhere to this timetable as intently as could really be expected. Break down what it means for your efficiency and productivity.

3. Wake-up routines

- Routine is Critical: Lay out a predictable wake-up routine that establishes the vibe for your day. This could incorporate exercises like journaling, contemplation, or a concise survey of your objectives.

- Careful Beginning: Move toward your morning schedule with care. Be completely present in every action, whether it's tasting your morning espresso or going for a run. This can assist with making a feeling of quiet and concentration.

4. The Impact of trained instinct

- Propensity Stacking: Integrate new propensities into your current morning schedule. For instance, in the event that you as of now clean your teeth toward the beginning of the day, stack another propensity like flossing onto it.

- Begin Little: Start with each or two new propensities in turn. Attempting to change an excess of excessively fast can overpower.

- Following Advancement: Keep a diary or use propensity following applications to screen your advancement. Commend your victories and gain from any difficulties.

- Activity Plan: Pick a couple of efficiency hacks that impact you and incorporate them into your morning schedule. Be predictable and patient as you conform to these changes.

By changing your attitude, coordinating activity into your morning, and executing efficiency hacks, you can completely change yourself in momentous ways. The key is to move toward these progressions with commitment and an eagerness to adjust to what turns out best for you. Recall that individual change is an excursion, and your morning schedule fills in as a strong impetus for this cycle.

CHAPTER 4.

CARE AND TAKING CARE OF ONESELF.

Taking care of oneself is a key part of keeping up with physical, mental, and close to home prosperity. In this segment, we will dig into the standards of taking care of oneself, zeroing in on both care and reflection, and investigate different taking care of oneself ceremonies that can assist you with beginning your day with a feeling of imperativeness.

Mindfulness and Reflection: Focusing Your Morning.

Care and reflection are integral assets for accomplishing a decent and amicable beginning to your day. They assist you develop a more profound association with yourself and your environment.

- Discovering a genuine sense of reconciliation and concentration.

1. Careful Mindfulness.

- The Force of Presence:
Care is the act of being completely present at the time. It includes recognizing your considerations, sentiments, and sensations without judgment.

- Careful Relaxing: A basic yet viable method for rehearsing care is through careful relaxing. Shut your eyes, take a couple of full breaths, and concentrate on the vibe of your breath as it enters and leaves your body.

- Appreciation Practice: Consider beginning your day with an appreciation practice. Think about the things you're thankful for and how they add to your prosperity.

- Activity Step: Tomorrow first thing, require a couple of moments to rehearse careful breathing or appreciation. Notice what it means for your state of mind and by and large standpoint.

- Rehearsing Care in day to day existence.

- Integrating Care into Day to day Exercises: Care doesn't need to be restricted to formal contemplation. You can implant care into regular undertakings, like having breakfast or cleaning up.

- Setting Expectations: Begin your day with clear expectations. What is it that you need to accomplish or encounter today? Setting positive aims can shape your day's direction.

- Careful Eating: While eating, give close consideration to the flavors and surfaces of your food. Eating carefully can assist you with appreciating your dinner and feel more fulfilled.

- Activity Plan: Distinguish a day to day action you can approach carefully. It very well may be your morning espresso, cleaning your teeth, or even your drive to work. Attempt to draw in with this movement in a completely present and non-critical manner.

Self care Customs for a Morning Shine.

Taking care of oneself customs are fundamental for sustaining your physical, mental, and profound wellbeing. These customs can assist you with developing a brilliant and positive beginning to your day.

- Sustaining Your Body and Soul

1. Morning Stretch and Development.

- Extending Schedule: Consolidating a delicate extending routine can empower your body and facilitate any solidness from rest. Center around regions like your neck, shoulders, and back to deliver pressure.

- Yoga Practice: Yoga offers a far reaching mind-body insight. Consider devoting a part of your morning to a short yoga meeting, which can further develop adaptability, strength, and mental clearness.

- Morning Walk: In the event that you have the open door, a morning stroll in the outside air can be a reviving encounter. It permits you to associate with nature and experience the quietness of early mornings.

- Activity Step: Tomorrow first thing, attempt a short extending routine or yoga practice. On the other hand, step outside for a short walk if conceivable. Focus on how your body and brain answer.

2. Morning Sustenance for Sustenance

- Adjusted Breakfast: Guarantee that your morning meal is a reasonable feast. Incorporate a mix of macronutrients, like protein, carbs, and solid fats. This gives supported energy to your morning.

- Hydration: Begin your day with a glass of water to rehydrate your body following a night's rest. You can likewise appreciate natural tea or a hydrating smoothie.

- Careful Eating: Having your morning meal carefully can upgrade your enthusiasm for the dinner and forestall gorging. Bite your food gradually and relish each nibble.

- Activity Plan: Think about making a nutritious breakfast a day to day taking care of oneself custom. Explore different avenues regarding different breakfast choices to find what leaves you feeling generally stimulated and fulfilled.

3. Individual Prosperity Practices

- Journaling: Journaling can be a helpful morning practice. Record your considerations, sentiments, or objectives. It's an open door to self-reflect and acquire lucidity.

- Certifications: Integrating positive insistences into your morning schedule can help your confidence and certainty. Rehashing certifications connected with taking care of oneself and self esteem can establish an inspirational vibe for the afternoon.

- Reflection: Contemplation doesn't need to be extended. Indeed, even a short contemplation practice can quiet your brain and increment your concentration and versatility for the day ahead.

- Activity Step: Explore different avenues regarding one of these individual prosperity rehearses in your morning schedule. Begin with a brief journaling meeting, certifications, or a short reflection. See what it means for your temperament and outlook.

By integrating care and reflection into your morning and embracing taking care of oneself ceremonies, you can support your body and soul, making way for a morning shine that stretches out over the course of your day. These practices can assist you with starting every day with a feeling of internal quiet and imperativeness, empowering you to explore life's difficulties with versatility and beauty.

CONCLUSION.

Sustaining Your Morning dominance: Tips for long-haul achievements.

Keeping up with morning predominance for the long haul requires predictable exertion and versatility. In this segment, we'll investigate systems to assist you with keeping focused and conform to life's changes.

- Remaining Reliable with your Daily schedule.

1. Everyday Ceremonies for Morning Strength

- Routine Advantages: Morning schedules give design and consistency. They set a mood for your day and make a feeling of solace and solidness.

- Receiving the Benefits: Consistency in your morning schedule prompts total advantages over the long run. You're bound to see improvement in regions like efficiency, prosperity, and self-improvement when you stay with your daily schedule.

- Activity Step: Think about your ongoing morning schedule. Are there components you've been steady with, and have you noticed enhancements in those areas? Consider any changes or increments that could additionally improve your everyday practice.

2. Responsibility and Backing

- Sharing Your Objectives: One method for keeping up with consistency is by offering your morning objectives to a confided in companion or relative. They can act as responsibility accomplices, empowering you to remain focused.

- Local area Backing: Joining a local area or gathering with comparable morning schedules can exceptionally spur. Whether it's a web-based gathering or a nearby get together, you can draw motivation from others and offer your advancement.

- Activity Plan: In the event that you haven't as of now, share your morning objectives with somebody you trust or consider joining a local area that lines up with your morning schedule interests.

Examine how this outside help can assist you with remaining steady.

*   Adjusting to Life's Progressions

1. Adaptability in Your Daily schedule

- Life's Dynamic Nature: Life is brimming with startling changes, for example, vocation shifts, family commitments, and self-improvements. Adaptability in your morning schedule permits you to adjust to these progressions while keeping up with your general objectives.

- Strength: Flexibility and strength are vital to long haul achievement. Rather than becoming dampened by interruptions, consider them to be potential chances to learn and develop.

- Activity Step: Survey any new changes in your day to day existence that have impacted your morning schedule. How could you adjust, and what did you gain from these changes? Recognize procedures to keep up with consistency during times of progress.

2. Survey and Change Your Objectives

- **Ordinary Evaluation:** Occasionally survey your morning schedule and objectives. Could it be said that they are as yet lined up with your ongoing needs and values? If not, it could be an ideal opportunity to adapt.

- Brilliant Objective Setting: Guarantee that your objectives are Explicit, Quantifiable, Attainable, Significant, and Time-bound. Savvy objectives give a reasonable guide to your morning schedule.

- Activity Plan: Find opportunity to evaluate your ongoing morning schedule and objectives. Are there any adjustments expected to more readily mirror your advancing yearnings? Reexamine your objectives as needs be.

The Day break of Your Changed Life

As you proceed with your excursion of morning predominance, it's fundamental to consider how far you've come and to outfit the perpetual power inside each part of your life.

- Thinking about Your Excursion

1. The Force of Reflection

- Thinking Back: Reflection is an instrument that permits you to think back on your excursion. Commend your triumphs and recognize your development, regardless of how little or critical.

- Appreciation: Offer thanks for the snapshots of satisfaction and learning you've encountered en route. Appreciation can improve your general feeling of prosperity.

- Activity Step: Take time every morning to consider your excursion. You can do this through journaling or basically sitting unobtrusively and contemplating your accomplishments and the examples you've learned.

2. Laying out New Objectives

- Persistent Development: The excursion of morning predominance is a continuous interaction. Whenever you've accomplished specific objectives, now is the ideal time to set new ones to proceed with your development and change.

- Developing Targets: As you progress, your objectives might develop. What was once a critical accomplishment could now be a venturing stone toward considerably more prominent goals.

- Activity Plan: Survey your ongoing objectives and consider what you need to accomplish straightaway. Are there new regions you might want to investigate in your morning normal and in your life in general?

- Embracing Unending Power in Each Part of Life.

1. Rising above Your Morning

- Adaptable Abilities: The abilities and mentality you've developed in your morning schedule can be applied to different parts of your life. The discipline, concentration, and positive reasoning you've created can impact your general prosperity.

- Comprehensive Change: Understand that your morning schedule is only one part of your comprehensive prosperity. Look for chances to apply the standards of morning predominance to various parts of your life, like work, connections, and self-improvement.

- Activity Step: Recognize one aspect of your life where you can apply the examples and abilities you've acquired from your morning schedule. This could be putting forth unambiguous business related objectives or working on your correspondence in connections.

2. Releasing Your True capacity

- Unending Development: Perceive that the force of personal growth is unlimited. Your morning schedule is an impetus for self-awareness, and this development can go on endlessly.

- Embrace Difficulties: Welcome difficulties and misfortunes as any open doors for learning and development. The more you face difficulties with strength and a development outlook, the more enabled you become.

- Activity Plan: Consider a test or obstruction you've experienced as of late. How might you reexamine it as a chance for self-improvement? Distinguish explicit moves toward explore this test with a development mentality.

By supporting your morning strength with consistency, flexibility, and an emphasis all things considered and development, you can open unending power inside yourself. Your morning schedule is an establishment for long lasting achievement and prosperity, and its standards can be applied to all parts of your life. Embrace the excursion, commend your accomplishments, and keep on laying out new objectives as you bridle the interminable power that lives inside you.

Permit me to stretch out my heartfelt thanks to You for choosing my book. In the event that you delighted in it, could you kindly think about leaving a review on amazon? Your review is basic to me and others searching for help connected with a similar book.